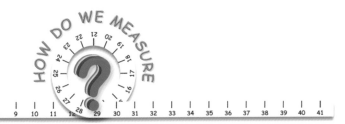

HOW DO WE MEASURE ?

Time

BLACKBIRCH PRESS

An imprint of Thomson Gale, a part of The Thomson Corporation

THOMSON

GALE

Detroit • New York • San Francisco • San Diego • New Haven, Conn. • Waterville, Maine • London • Munich

Consultant: Kimi Hosoume
Associate Director of GEMS (Great
    Explorations in Math and Science),
Director of PEACHES (Primary
    Explorations for Adults, Children,
    and Educators in Science),
Lawrence Hall of Science,
University of California,
Berkeley, California

For The Brown Reference Group plc
Text: Chris Woodford
Project Editor: Lesley Campbell-Wright
Designer: Lynne Ross
Picture Researcher: Susy Forbes
Illustrators: Darren Awuah and Mark Walker
Managing Editor: Bridget Giles
Children's Publisher: Anne O'Daly
Production Director: Alastair Gourlay
Editorial Director: Lindsey Lowe

PHOTOGRAPHIC CREDITS
Anthroarcheart.org: 10; **The Brown Reference Group plc:** 11, Edward Allwright, 28, 29,
Martin Norris, 25b; **Casio:** 25t, 26; **Corbis:** Archivo Iconografico S. A. 13, Bettmann 20, Pablo
Corral 16, Jack Hollingsworth 24; **NASA:** 18, 21, 27t; **National Maritime Museum:** 17;
Photos.com: 1, 7, 22, 27b; **Rex Features:** Dan Charity (SON/NAP) 8, Henryk T. Kaiser 12;
SPL: John Sanford 4–5.

Front cover: **The Brown Reference Group plc:** Edward Allwright

LIBRARY OF CONGRESS CATALOGING-IN-PUBLICATION DATA

Woodford, Chris.
  Time / by Chris Woodford.
    p. cm. — (How do we measure?)
  Includes bibliographical references and index.
  ISBN 1-4103-0363-2 (hardcover) — ISBN 1-4103-0519-8 (pbk. : alk. paper)
  1. Time measurements—Juvenile literature. I. Title II. Series: Woodford, Chris.
How do we measure?

  QB213.W66 2005
  529'.7—dc22

                              2004016228

Printed and bound in Thailand
10 9 8 7 6 5 4 3 2 1

Contents

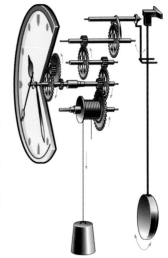

What is time?

Each birthday, you become one year older. You do not get older just on your birthdays, though. You get a little bit older every day. Time is how we mark the rate at which we age.

We cannot see time, but it is always there. Although time is invisible, we can measure it with watches and clocks.

Earth, Moon, and Sun

Our ideas about time come from the way Earth, the Moon, and the Sun move in the sky. It takes a year for Earth to circle the Sun. It takes about a month for the Moon to move around Earth. All this time Earth is also spinning very slowly like a top. It takes 24 hours for Earth to spin once. We feel it is day when our part of Earth faces the Sun and night when our part of Earth faces away from the Sun.

It takes about a month for the Moon to move once around Earth. The shape of the Moon changes throughout the month. A crescent Moon is a thin slice. A full Moon is a full circle.

Crescent Moon ⟶ *Full Moon*

Passing seasons

Earth turns around an imaginary line called an axis. The axis leans slightly to one side. As Earth revolves around the Sun, the Northern Hemisphere, or northern half of Earth, tilts toward the Sun at some times of the year (**1**) and away from the Sun at the other times (**2**). When the Northern Hemisphere tilts toward the Sun, it has summer because there are more hours of daylight. The Sun is also higher in the sky, making the sunlight stronger and warmer.

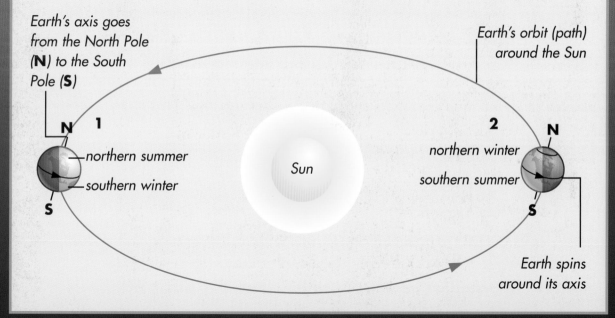

Earth's axis goes from the North Pole (**N**) to the South Pole (**S**)

Earth's orbit (path) around the Sun

1

northern summer

southern winter

Sun

2

northern winter

southern summer

Earth spins around its axis

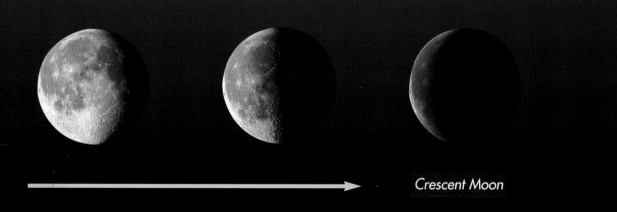

Crescent Moon

Units of time

Time goes on forever. To make it easier to measure, we divide it into smaller pieces, or units. The biggest unit of time is an eon. An eon is such a long period of time that it cannot even be measured. Another large unit of time is called a millennium. A millennium is the name we give to 1,000 years. Besides years, there are months, weeks, days, hours, minutes, and seconds.

The tiniest unit of time scientists can measure is called a picosecond. Imagine a second divided into a million equal

How much time?

15 billion years =	*age of the Universe*
4.5 billion years =	*age of Earth*
75 years =	*average life of a person*
22 months =	*time it takes for a baby elephant to grow inside its mother*
365 days =	*time it takes for Earth to go around the Sun*
8 hours =	*amount of sleep most adults need each night*
8 minutes =	*time it takes for light to travel from the Sun to Earth*
1 second =	*beat of a human heart*
1 tenth of a second =	*time it takes to blink*
1 millisecond =	*one-thousandth of a second; time for a camera lens to snap open*

pieces. (A million is 1,000,000.) Then imagine one of those tiny pieces divided up into a million even smaller pieces. That is how long a picosecond lasts.

Clocks measure time in hours, minutes, and seconds. This clock is an alarm clock. When the alarm goes off, the hammer at the top of the clock moves back and forth. It hits the bells to make a loud noise.

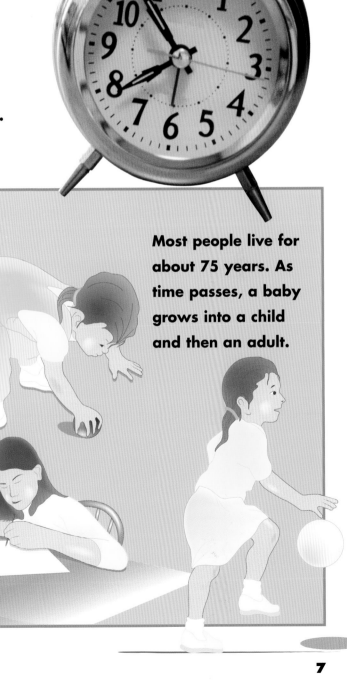

Most people live for about 75 years. As time passes, a baby grows into a child and then an adult.

Time and the ancients

People who lived thousands of years ago did not have watches or clocks. Even so, they had ways to measure time. The ancient Egyptians invented sundials, which tell time using the Sun. When the Sun shines on the sundial's pointer, it casts a shadow onto the dial (round face). The dial is marked with the hours, from one to twelve. As the Sun moves around the sky, the shadow moves around the dial, just like the hour hand of a clock.

Other ways to tell time

Sundials are not very accurate and do not work at night. So ancient people had to

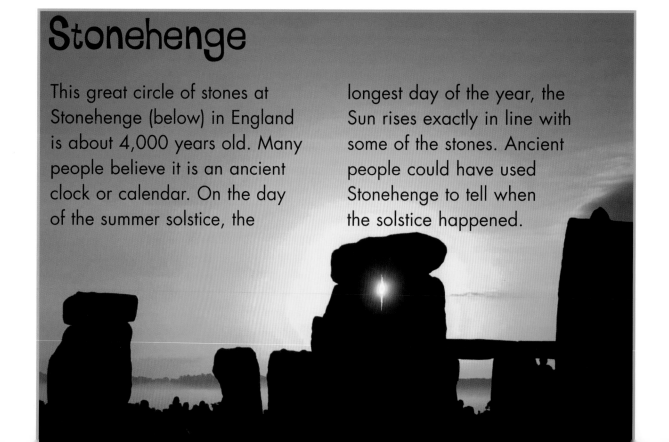

Stonehenge

This great circle of stones at Stonehenge (below) in England is about 4,000 years old. Many people believe it is an ancient clock or calendar. On the day of the summer solstice, the longest day of the year, the Sun rises exactly in line with some of the stones. Ancient people could have used Stonehenge to tell when the solstice happened.

think of other ways to tell time. Some things always take the same amount of time to happen. Ancient people used this idea to measure time.

In an hourglass, for example, it takes exactly one hour for a fixed amount of sand to trickle from the top half of the hourglass to the bottom half. Ancient people could measure each passing hour by turning over an hourglass.

An hourglass and other early timepieces, such as an Egyptian water clock, are shown below.

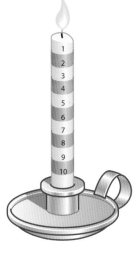

Candle clock
As a candle clock burned down, people could count the number of hours that had passed.

Hourglass
It takes exactly one hour for the sand to trickle from the top to the bottom of this hourglass.

Oil clock
People could tell the time using an oil clock by the amount of oil that burned away in the lamp.

Egyptian water clock
Water drips slowly from a hole in a pot and shows how many hours have passed.

Calendars

Besides measuring the hours in a day, ancient people also needed calendars to keep track of the days in a year. Nearly 2,500 years ago, people who lived in Babylon, in what is now Iraq, used the Moon to create the first calendars. They saw that the Moon took about 29.5 days to complete a cycle from one full Moon to another. They called this time a month.

A better calendar

Their year had 12 of these months, which gave a total of 354 days. Their calendar was not exact, though. A year really has 365 days.

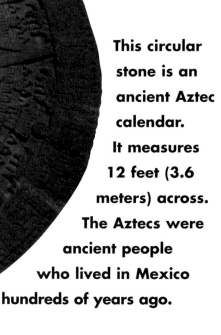

This circular stone is an ancient Aztec calendar. It measures 12 feet (3.6 meters) across. The Aztecs were ancient people who lived in Mexico hundreds of years ago.

February 2004

Mon	Tues	Wed	Thur	Fri	Sat	Sun
						1
2	3	4	5	6	7	8
9	10	11	12	13	14	15
16	17	18	19	20	21	22
23	24	25	26	27	28	29

Every four years there is a leap year. In a leap year, February has 29 days instead of the usual 28 days.

Thousands of years ago the ancient Egyptians made a better calendar using the Sun. They figured out how long Earth took to move around the Sun. They called that time a year.

The Egyptians divided their year into 12 to make the months. Each month had 30 days. The ancient Egyptians added five extra days at the end of the year to make a total of 365 days.

Leap years

In the modern calendar, a year has 365 days. But Earth really takes a little longer than this to go once around the Sun: 365 days, 5 hours, 48 minutes, and 46 seconds, to be exact. If every year had only 365 days, our calendars would soon fall out of step with the Sun. So our calendars add an extra day—February 29—every four years. These slightly longer years have 366 days and are called leap years.

The pendulum

Imagine if you had to go outside to look at a sundial whenever you wanted to know the time, or if you had to fill up a water clock so you would be on time for school. Early clocks like these were not very useful.

In the 17th century, a famous Italian scientist named Galileo (1564–1642) invented the pendulum. A pendulum is a long bar with a heavy weight at one end.

Controlling a clock

If a pendulum is kept swinging, it always takes the same amount of time to swing back and forth. That makes a pendulum useful to help tell time. Galileo suggested using a swinging pendulum to control how a clock works.

A swing works like a pendulum. Like a pendulum, the girl will swing in a regular pattern.

Pendulums, Galileo, and gravity

Galileo was fascinated by gravity.
He got the idea for the pendulum
while he was watching a lamp
swinging in the cathedral in
Pisa, Italy. When he timed the
swings using the pulse in his
wrist, he found the lamp always
took exactly the same time to
move back and forth.

Gravity is the force that makes
things fall toward Earth. It also
keeps Earth and the other planets
moving around the Sun. Gravity
also makes a pendulum swing.

**Galileo invented the pendulum
after watching a swinging lamp.**

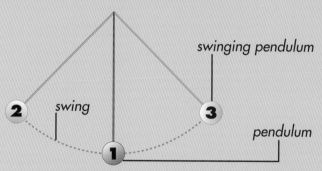

swinging pendulum

swing

pendulum

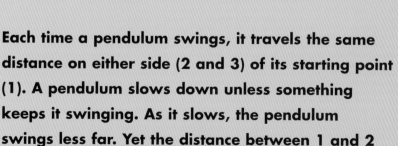

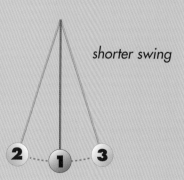

shorter swing

**Each time a pendulum swings, it travels the same
distance on either side (2 and 3) of its starting point
(1). A pendulum slows down unless something
keeps it swinging. As it slows, the pendulum
swings less far. Yet the distance between 1 and 2
and between 1 and 3 always remains the same.**

Gears and springs

Pendulum clocks are mechanical. They have lots of moving parts. Some of the most important parts are called gears. Gears are wheels with jagged teeth cut into their edges. The gears make a clock's hands turn. The swinging pendulum controls how fast the gears move. A slowly falling weight powers the clock. Pendulum clocks have problems. The pendulum may change length slightly in hot or cold weather. That makes the clock run too fast or too slow. The clock also has to be kept still so the pendulum swings properly.

Spring power

18th-century clockmakers found another way to drive their clocks. Instead of using a falling weight, they used springs. These little spirals of wire power a clock and keep it ticking at an exact rate as they unwind.

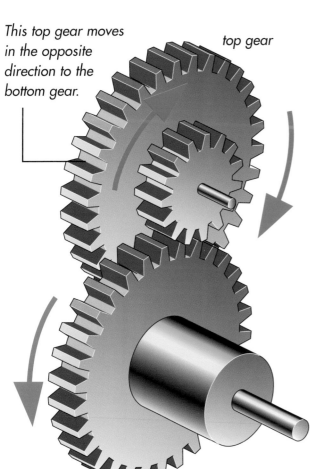

This top gear moves in the opposite direction to the bottom gear.

top gear

bottom gear

In a mechanical clock, the gears turn the clock's hands around at a precise speed.

Inside a pendulum clock

When a pendulum swings, it rocks a lever called a pallet. The pallet lifts up and down once every second. This makes a "tick-tock" noise. As the pallet moves, it turns the escape wheel. This wheel is connected by gears to other wheels, including the main wheel.

Falling weight

The main wheel has a heavy weight fixed to it that slowly moves down. The falling weight powers the clock by turning the main wheel. The main wheel then turns the other gears. The swinging pendulum controls the movement of these gears. The gears turn the hands around the dial. The clock has to be wound regularly by winding the cord back around the barrel to raise the weight.

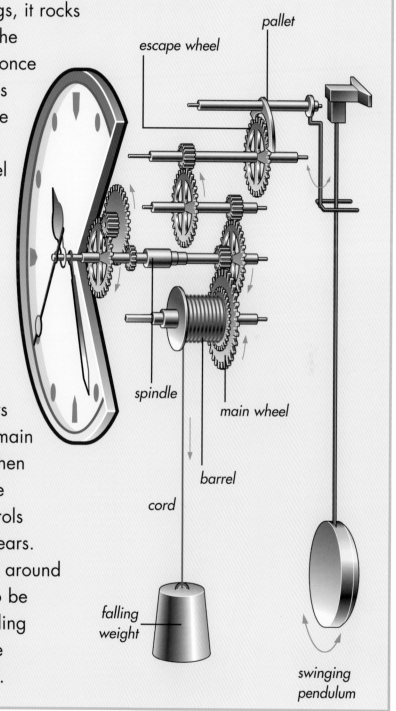

pallet

escape wheel

spindle

main wheel

barrel

cord

falling weight

swinging pendulum

From clocks to watches

Early clocks were large and expensive. They were large because of their long, swinging pendulums. They were expensive because clockmakers had to cut each gear wheel by hand.

Some clockmakers used very smooth jewels, such as diamonds, for some of the moving parts. Clocks with

This clockmaker is using an eyepiece to see the tiny parts inside a watch.

Clocks at sea

Early mechanical clocks were fine on land but could not be used on ships. The tumbling waves of the sea made it impossible for a pendulum to swing properly. A British clockmaker named John Harrison (1693–1776) eventually solved the problem of how to tell time at sea. He built very accurate sea clocks driven by special springs. One was a large pocket watch called H4. It was so well made that it lost only five seconds during a sea voyage from England to Jamaica in 1762.

John Harrison made his first sea clock, called H1, between 1730 and 1735 in England.

jewels kept better time, but jewels are expensive.

Invention of springs

For a long time, clocks were large, luxury items and few people could afford them. The invention of springs allowed clockmakers to make smaller clocks and watches without pendulums and falling weights. In 1841 a British engineer named Joseph Whitworth (1803–1887) invented a machine that cut gears. Soon small clocks and watches could be made in factories. These watches and clocks were inexpensive, so more people could buy them.

Time zones

When you are having breakfast in the morning, somewhere else in the world other people are having dinner. Everyone agrees what time it is using time zones. The world is divided into 24 time zones. People living in each zone have their own time.

Greenwich Mean Time

Everyone's time is set by the time at Greenwich

A picture of Earth taken from the Moon. Only one side of Earth faces the Sun at any time. It is daytime on the side that faces the Sun. It is nighttime on the other side. As Earth spins around its axis, different parts of Earth face the Sun.

in London, England. The time there is called Greenwich Mean Time (GMT). People living in time zones east of Greenwich have later times than GMT. People living in time zones west of Greenwich have earlier times.

From Pacific coast to Atlantic coast

North America is such a big continent that it has five different time zones. The time is always three hours later in the day for New Yorkers than it is for Californians. That is because the Sun rises earlier over New York than over California.

Daylight saving time

During summer, the days are longer and the nights are shorter. Some countries and states change their time systems so people can enjoy long summer evenings. In spring, everyone puts their clocks forward by one hour so it gets dark one hour later. In fall, people set their clocks back again. This system is called daylight saving time.

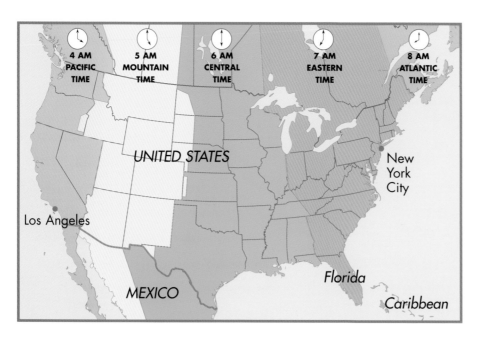

North America has five different time zones. When it is noon in New York City, it is only 9 a.m. on the west coast in Los Angeles, California.

Time and speed

When you feel bored, time seems to pass slowly. When you are having fun, time seems to speed by. That is a trick of the mind—time almost always passes at the same speed.

But a brilliant German-born American scientist named Albert Einstein (1879–1955) showed that sometimes time can speed up or slow down.

Traveling at the speed of light

Light travels at the incredibly fast speed of 186,000 miles (298,000 km) each second. Suppose you could sit on a beam of light and zoom along with it. Einstein said that time would pass more slowly for you traveling on that beam of light than for people who were not moving so fast.

Theory of relativity

Einstein's ideas are called the theory of relativity. His ideas are very important and made people think about time and space in completely new ways.

Famous scientist Albert Einstein was born in Germany but became an American citizen. Einstein's ideas showed that the faster an object travels through space, the slower it travels through time!

Time-traveling twins

Einstein wondered how different people would measure time if they traveled at different speeds. Imagine a pair of identical twins. One twin stays on Earth. The other twin steps into a space rocket and blasts off into space (right). She travels around the solar system at nearly the speed of light. Then she comes back to Earth. Einstein said time would slow down for the astronaut twin because of her fast speed. So when she got back to Earth, she would be younger than her twin sister.

Although a rocket travels through space much faster than a train, the rocket moves more slowly through time.

ROCKET:
faster speed
slower time

TRAIN:
slower speed
faster time

Earth time

Clocks and watches measure the hours in a day. Calendars help us keep track of the months and years. How can we measure even longer periods of time? Suppose scientists want to know how old a dinosaur bone is. There is no clock they can look at to tell them.

A fossil of a pterodactyl. Pterodactyls lived 144 to 65 million years ago. Scientists can figure out how old a fossil is by using carbon dating.

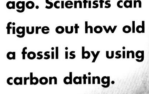

HOW A FOSSIL FORMS

1. Millions of years ago, a dinosaur dies next to a river.

1.

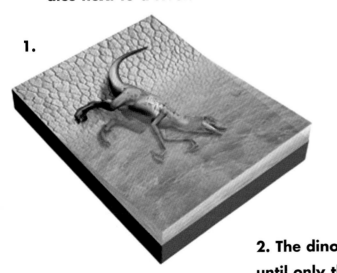

2.

2. The dinosaur's flesh rots, until only the bones are left. The river covers these bones in mud.

American chemist William Libby (1908–1980) discovered the answer in 1947. He found that he could figure out how old something was by measuring how much carbon it contained. Libby called this method carbon dating.

Fossils are the remains of long-dead creatures that have turned to stone. The age of rocks and fossils can be determined by measuring how much carbon the fossils contain.

Carbon clock

Everything that has ever lived contains some carbon. It is the black material in coal and in pencil "lead." Over millions of years, carbon changes into another kind of carbon. The change happens very slowly but at a steady rate. The changing carbon in living or dead things is like a slowly ticking clock. By measuring the different amounts of carbon present, a scientist can figure out how old something is.

3.

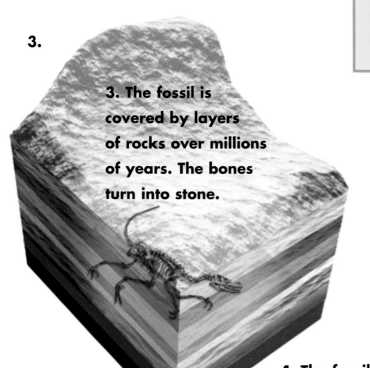

3. The fossil is covered by layers of rocks over millions of years. The bones turn into stone.

4.

4. The fossil is found when the rocks wear away. It can then be carbon dated.

Modern clocks

Modern clocks and watches are not powered by falling weights or springs. They run on batteries, or electric power. A tiny battery makes the electricity to keep the watch going. Some clocks and watches use a tiny piece of quartz to tell the time.

Quartz is a type of crystal. When electricity flows into it, the crystal shakes back and forth at a precise rate. Quartz watches use this shaking movement to keep track of the time.

This girl's modern digital wristwatch does not have a clock face and moving hands to tell the time. Instead, it shows the time using numbers, or digits.

Digital watches

Some people still tell time with watches and clocks that have moving hands. Other people, though, prefer digital clocks and watches.

Digital clocks like the one shown here show the time with numbers, or digits. They often have a built-in stopwatch and alarm clock. Some watches may also show the time in different countries. Inside a digital watch, there is usually a piece of quartz crystal to keep time.

This digital alarm clock runs on electricity. It contains a battery and a piece of quartz to power it.

It takes very little energy to make quartz move. So the battery in a quartz watch can last for many years.

The first quartz clock was made in 1928 by American engineers Joseph Horton and Warren Marrison.

This boy is using a stopwatch to time how long it takes him to do something. Modern stopwatches are digital. They do not have a clock face. Instead, digits show the time (as on the alarm clock above).

Tomorrow's time

Once people told time by looking at the skies. In the last few hundred years, clockmakers have found much better methods of measuring time.

These methods include pendulums and weights, spring-driven clocks, and digital watches. How will people tell time in the future?

The most accurate way of telling time now is with an atomic clock. An atomic clock works like a super-accurate quartz clock.

Instead of quartz, an atomic clock uses tiny atoms, or particles. These atoms give off pulses of energy ten billion times every second. The clock counts these pulses to tell the time.

This is no ordinary wristwatch. As well as telling the time, it lets you find out where you are on Earth with its global positioning system, or GPS. GPS uses space satellites and stations on the ground to figure out exactly where you are in the world.

These numbers tell the wearer exactly where she or he is.

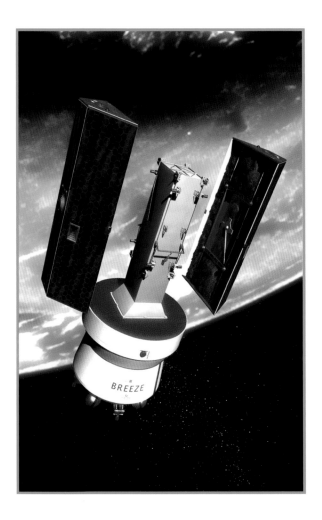

Biological clocks

We all have a built-in sense of time. Even without looking at a clock, we know when we feel sleepy or hungry. That is called our biological clock. Scientists think our biological clocks are driven by proteins. Proteins are the chemicals from which our bodies are made. In the future, scientists will find out much more about biological clocks.

Plants have biological clocks that tell them when to flower.

A GPS satellite orbits, or goes around, Earth hundreds of miles above the ground in space. GPS satellites carry atomic clocks that measure the time exactly.

An atomic clock is so accurate that it loses just one second every 30,000 years. Perhaps in the future we will all wear miniature atomic clocks on our wrists!

Make a sundial

1 Put the plate on top of the cardboard. Draw around the edge of the plate to make a circle on the cardboard.

You will need:

- A piece of thin cardboard about 12 inches (30 cm) by 12 inches (30 cm)
- A sharp pencil
- A dinner plate about 10 inches (25 cm) across
- Modeling clay
- Scissors

2 Cut out the circle using the scissors. Get an adult to help you. Be very careful with the scissors.

3 Figure out roughly where the center of the circle is. Make a small pencil mark there.

4 Put a small ball of modeling clay on the underside of the cardboard beneath the pencil mark.

5

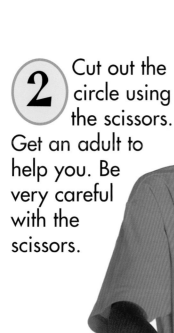

5 Carefully push the pencil through the center of the cardboard so it goes through the modeling clay. Ask an adult to help you. Try not to bend the cardboard.

6 Place your sundial on the ground outside. Choose somewhere that will be in the Sun all day.

Your finished sundial

Once you have drawn the hour lines for 3, 6, 9, and 12 o'clock, you can figure out where the other hour lines go by dividing each quarter of the circle into equal thirds.

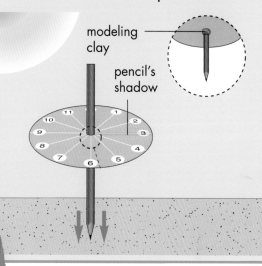

modeling clay

pencil's shadow

7 At noon, draw a straight line where the pencil's shadow falls. Do the same at 3 o'clock and 6 o'clock in the afternoon, and at 9 o'clock in the morning.

Glossary _____

atom A tiny particle of a substance.

atomic clock A very accurate clock that tells time using the tiny movements of atoms.

biological clock An animal's or plant's built-in sense of time.

calendar A way of keeping track of the days, weeks, and months in a year.

carbon dating A way of finding out the age of very old things, such as rocks and fossils.

day and night The time it takes for Earth to spin once.

daylight saving time Setting the clock forward one hour to make the most of long summer days.

digital watch A watch that shows the time with numbers, not hands.

escape wheel The main driving wheel in a pendulum clock.

gear A pair of joined wheels with teeth around their edges.

The wheels turn at different speeds depending on how many teeth each has.

mechanical clock A clock that is made of moving parts, such as gears, pendulums, and springs.

month The approximate time it takes for the Moon to go once around Earth.

pendulum A swinging bar that helps keep time in a mechanical clock.

picosecond One million millionth of a second.

quartz clock A modern clock that uses the movements of quartz to keep time.

relativity A theory by Albert Einstein; in relativity, time slows down when people travel at very high speeds.

solstice The day of the year with the longest daylight hours is the summer solstice (June 21). The winter solstice (December 22) is the shortest day of the year.

spring a spiral of wire that powers a mechanical clock.

sundial A device that measures time using shadows.

time zone A region of the world that has the same time.

year The time it takes for Earth to move once around the Sun (365 days).

Find out more

Books

Betty Maestro, *The Story of Clocks and Calendars.* London: HarperCollins, 1999.

Clare Seymour, *Inside a Clock.* Danbury, CN: Grolier/ Scholastic Library, 2001.

James Dunbar, *Tick-Tock.* Minneapolis, MN.: Lerner Publications, 1998.

John Gribben and Mary Gribben, *Eyewitness Time and Space.* London: Dorling Kindersley, 2000.

Louise Borden, *Sea Clocks: The Story of Longitude.* New York: McElderry, 2004.

Trent Duffy, *Turning Point Inventions: Clock.* Barcelona, Spain: Atheneum, 2000.

Web sites

How Stuff Works: Inside a Wind-up Alarm Clock
See how an alarm clock works
home.howstuffworks.com/ inside-clock.htm

It's About Time
Learn all about the past, the present, and the future
www.units.muohio.edu/ dragonfly/time

Official U.S. Time
Shows the time in different parts of the United States
www.time.gov

Playing with Time
Lots of fun exhibits and activities to do with time
www.playingwithtime.org

World Time Server
What time is it around the world?
www.worldtimeserver.com

Index